# FITNESS IS LIFE
# AND
# LIFE IS FITNESS

---

*How Reaching My Fitness Goals Taught Me*

*the Method for Reaching Any Goal in Life*

---

**BY CARL HUNTER**

# Acknowledgments

I would like to thank the following people:

**Audra Mary Wilson** for her encouragements to share my story.

All But Dissertation (ABD) **Angela Spencer** (soon to be Angela Spencer, PhD) for being analytical and requiring that I defend the encouragements I shared.

**Catherine Egboh** for bringing a youthful opinion and ensuring I remembered that words matter.

# Is This Book for You?

This book is for you if you are interested in changing something about yourself. I will share with you how the techniques I have utilized to successfully change my fitness are the same techniques I have utilized to successfully change other aspects of my life. This book is partly autobiographical and partly self-help. Autobiographical, because I share my personal stories and experiences to illustrate my encouragements; self-help, if you find something I share helpful for you becoming a better you.

This book may help you if one or more of the following is true:

- You are interested in discovering a consistent method for changing something about yourself.

- You want to change some aspect of your life but you don't know how to get started.

- After you start changing something about yourself you get discouraged and overwhelmed when you realize there is much more to it than you imagined.

- You tend to overestimate your abilities while underestimating the challenges of changing yourself.

- You want to change something about yourself, but you are afraid to fail.

# How You Can Use This Book

I wrote this book to share how I made the difficult effort of changing myself more structural and consistent. In order for you to discover the structure I used to change my fitness or any aspect of my life, all you have to do is to read the chapters in order.

Each chapter builds on the previous chapter, and each chapter addresses an element of the change structure and offers the methods I use to apply it. You'll learn how I get consistent results in both fitness and other aspects of my life, and by applying what you've learned, you can start to see results in your life too.

# Table of Contents

# Introduction

Many years ago, I witnessed an awesome event. I was eight years old, maybe nine, and my father told me that I had to help him clean up "stuff" which had accumulated outside at the back of our house. I am sure you can imagine, like most nine year old boys, I did not want to help because I had a hundred other things I wanted to do. I reluctantly went with my father; after all, you know I really didn't have a choice. As we were moving stuff from one pile to another, we happened upon a pipe. As I recall, it was similar to a concrete pressure pipe or maybe a metal pipe for plumbing. I'm not sure, but I do remember it was dark green and black and a little rusty looking. It was buried in the dirt on one end and was about three or four feet in length and two feet in diameter, with squared ends.

I remember this because I saw my father grab the pipe with both hands, one hand on each end, and without any hesitation and very little effort, toss it aside as if it was nothing. It was only after I attempted to lift the pipe myself that I realized it was SUPER HEAVY! That pipe was so heavy I could only lift one end of it about two or three inches off the ground. Trust me, I put my whole body into the effort.

I knew I had just witnessed something amazing! It was official, my father was awesome! That was the first time I remember thinking that about my father. I stared at my father as he continued moving stuff, and he made no acknowledgment of what just happened and how incredible it was. My father noticed me staring at him and said to me what he had been saying all day, "Boy, get to work." However, this time, it was different: I actually wanted to get to work because this time was also the first time I realized I wanted to be just like him.

I witnessed my father's feat of strength over forty-five years ago, and this was the first time I was inspired to want to change myself to be different, to be better than I was. Although I didn't think of it at the time, my first fitness goal was to become strong just like my dad. From this first fitness

2

goal and with each subsequent goal, over the years, health and fitness became an integral part of my life. As I successfully achieved my fitness goals, I realized I could change any aspect of my life by utilizing the methods I used to change my fitness. Now I use these methods to help other people as well.

In my work as a Fitness Consultant, people frequently ask me questions starting with "How can I…?" Over time, I have become better at answering these questions based on people's answers to a series of questions I ask. I try to get a sense of "why" the person desires to do whatever they are asking me about. Similar to my story I just shared, I know the answer to why a client desires a change is in their story. From our first conversation and through all subsequent conversations, I am interested in getting to know more of their story and getting to know the reasons why they are pursuing their goal. After all, for me, getting to know someone's story is indeed the *personal* in personal fitness.

I am also *personally* invested in helping my clients succeed and reach their goals. Anytime my clients reach a milestone or achieve a goal, it reminds me of the pride and accomplishment I felt when I attained my first fitness goal. I am rewarded with a sense of achievement and professional satisfaction from their success. I can also be sensitive to the challenges my clients face and can help them identify their motivation for continuing toward their goal. I have faced fitness challenges myself and have come to realize that the more reasons a client has for their goal, the higher the probability of achieving the goal.

I stay connected to and humbled by my challenges when remembering my stories, such as the one I just shared with you. No matter where I find myself in life, remembering my stories reminds me where I came from and the struggles I overcame to get to where I am now.

These are the major reasons why I became a Fitness Consultant. However, somewhere along the way, I also discovered something unexpected and profound. I discovered that fitness is life and life is fitness, literally and figuratively.

Life has many aspects. Life is familial, life is educational, life is spiritual, life is social, life is career, life is health, life is fitness, and life is everything, and everything in life changes. Regardless of whether my desire to change is for fitness or for another aspect of my life, there is symmetry and sameness in regard to how I change.

4

For this reason, this book is not about fitness as it relates to working out, losing weight, or creating exercise programs, diets, or nutrition programs or the like. **This book is about life and how everything in life changes.** Most importantly, this book is about how fitness, a single aspect of my life, helped me recognize that change has a pattern and structure, and when I adhere to the pattern and structure of change, it makes my effort to change more efficient and effective. I hope that by sharing my story with you, you will learn how to apply what I have discovered and make life-changing, lasting improvements to your life as well.

# CHAPTER 1

*Who Am I, Where Am I Currently, and Where Do I Want to Go?*

Did you know that whether you consciously plan your life or you just live day to day without any real goal, you will still end up somewhere? Why not make it somewhere you want to be, a better place than you are now, instead of floating along and winding up somewhere you never really wanted to be in the first place? Think it can't happen? You may be there now, so let me tell you a little story about how I almost found myself there too.

One day, seemingly out of nowhere, a thought occurred to me. My thought was that I wanted a baby; more specifically, I wanted a daughter. Over the course of weeks, this thought continued to visit me and matured as I began to imagine having five or six babies. My daughter would be the oldest, and the others would be both boys and girls two or three years apart. I also imagined having a wife; however, truth be told, having a wife was secondary. My primary focus was the babies.

As time passed, my thought matured even further, and I began to imagine my life with my babies. I can remember a recurring and imagined fondness where it was dinnertime, and I was sitting at the head of the table. My babies were flanking me on both sides, and my wife sat at the other end of the table. I imagined my children's ages ranged from thirteen years old down to about four years old. The dining room was loud because my babies were all talking at the same time. One baby was irritating the other one, and one was screaming about something, while yet another was unconcerned with it all. The room was filled with the sounds of my children. As my wife was bringing dinner to the table, I asked one of my babies a question, such as, "How was school?" or "What did you and your friend do today?" I ensured that I acknowledged each child, making them the center of my attention. It was family time. At some point, I tasted the food and thought it was delicious. I would then say to my babies, "Tell your mama the food tastes good," and they would all say, "Mama, the food tastes good." Of course, they didn't say it in unison, and the younger children would only say a word or two in their cute little baby voices. Their mother then pleasingly responded. I then said to my babies, "Tell your mama to bring me something sweet." Again, they would say, "Mama, Daddy said to bring him something sweet!" My wife knew what "something sweet" meant, and she came to me and gave me a little peck on the lips, to which my babies laughed with happiness and excitement exclaiming, "Ooooooh, Mama kissed Daddy!" I was sixteen years old when I imagined this. I decided that in order to get my babies, my solution was simple. All I needed was two things: a job first, then a pretty girl to marry.

What do you imagine I knew at the age of sixteen about having six children? The answer… nothing! Was I naïve? Of course I was! The fact of the matter is that I had no idea of the reality of having six children. To this day, I cannot tell you why I came to desire six children; I just did. Back then, knowing "why" was not that important to me. What was more important was that I imagined it, came to desire it, and created a plan to acquire it. Most importantly, I remember being extremely confident and optimistic about it. At that time in my life, most of the time, I did not know why I was thinking, feeling, or desiring what I did. It was just the way it was.

You may have gathered from the story that earlier in my life, my decisions were desire based and my thoughts and actions were unstructured and not well thought-out or planned. Further, when my desire was strong enough, I was willing to change my life in a profound way with no real thoughts or concerns of the grand scheme of my life.

Thankfully, my simplistic plan turned out to be much more complicated than I thought, and I did not have six children. A few years later when I was more mature, I realized the responsibility of six children and thought to myself, "Carl, you dodged a bullet!" This near miss made me realize that not every desire that seemed good *to* me was good *for* me. I decided I would no longer live or change my life in a haphazard way.

I knew I needed to figure out a better way, a way where the major changes I made in my life were based on thoughts, desires, and decisions which were thought-out, well planned, and had structure.

Over time, a pattern emerged showing me how I could gain consistency for changes I wanted to make in my life. This pattern consisted of a series of thought processes that when organized, created my internal personal foundation, or what I refer to as my ***basic self***.

9

In order to help me explain my basic self, let's consider your car. Every day when you wake up and before you decide to drive anywhere, you have an idea of the capabilities of your car. You know things such as the age of your car and if it is brand new or very old. You know its mechanical condition, if the check engine light is on or if you have performed all the regularly scheduled maintenance. You know the condition of the tires and if there are any fluid leaks under the car. You are aware of whether your car starts immediately or if you have to cross your fingers and hope it will start. You derive your *basic car* definition from this type of information as well as your experiences with your car. Your *basic car* definition indicates the confidence you have in your car. Your basic car definition helps you decide if you will drive your car only within walking distance from your home or to the grocery store; if you will drive it to the airport for that important flight or to the hospital for the birth of your first child; or if you will drive 1,400 miles from Austin, Texas, to Lansing, Michigan, for a new career opportunity.

My definition of my basic self is similar, whereas I derive it from my life experiences and other information about myself. My basic self is who I am every day I wake up, before I decide to do or change anything in my life. My basic self indicates my self-confidence, assesses who I am as a person and where I currently am in my life and, most importantly, helps me gauge my ability to do the things I want to do in my life.

## *I Define My Basic Self by Answering These Two (2) Questions:*

### **1. *Who Am I at This Point in My Life?***

I must endeavor to know myself before I change myself.

Before I pursue any fitness or life endeavor, it is crucial for me to know myself, in order to be true to myself before I attempt to change myself. I acknowledge that my life is dynamic and change is inevitable, so the definition of my basic self must also be dynamic.

Change can also be expected or unexpected. Sometimes, things change for good, and sometimes, things change for bad. The source for change can come from within me or from an external source. In order to prepare for and respond to change, I accept that regardless of how change occurs in my life, before I take the first step to respond to it, I have to know who I am as a person and where I am currently in my life. Most importantly, I have learned that change has structure. Over time, and as I have matured, my thoughts, desires, and focus regarding how I change my life have become more holistic in nature.

Let me illustrate my meaning as it relates to fitness. As a Fitness Consultant, before I can design a fitness program for a client, I must perform a fitness assessment evaluation. The fitness assessment helps me get a sense of the person in terms of their fitness goal and their current fitness level.

The fitness assessment can be comprised of a battery of tests to determine the client's readiness for change. Are there any health concerns, injuries, or medications? What are their age and current maximum strength level? What about their muscular endurance, flexibility, and agility? What are their motivation level and availability to train? Can their reasons for wanting to change their fitness sustain their motivation to persevere when obstacles present? These considerations as well as others give me an idea of the client's readiness and ability to change their fitness condition.

After reviewing the results of the assessment with the client, we can work together to create a fitness plan that takes into account their strengths and weaknesses. My goal is to create a program the client agrees with and will perform consistently. I must design a fitness program that preserves and utilizes their strengths while reasonably challenging the client to improve their weaknesses. Most importantly, I must take into account who the person currently is in terms of being a fitness client and their current abilities, and offer ways to progress him or her toward their desired fitness change.

Determining *who I am* or knowing myself is similar and applies to all aspects of my life. For example, if I want to invest in the stock market, before I make my first investment, I have to determine who I am as an investor. In order for me to determine this, I have to assess my risk tolerance for losing my money. Am I a conservative investor, preferring to preserve my money with low-risk investments? Am I a moderately aggressive investor, willing to accept a bit more risk of losing my money in order to obtain a moderate return? Am I an aggressive investor, accepting a high risk of losing my money in order to obtain higher returns? Who I am as an investor predicts the future investment decisions I will make in the stock market.

It is reasonable to say that if I am conservative, I will pursue investments that preserve my money. However, if I disregard who I am as an investor and make investments contrary to being true to myself, the probability is high that the investment decisions I make may present unexpected consequences and repercussions. Further still, when I don't take the time to determine who I am as an investor, it opens the door to fear and doubt, which could derail my desire to invest or lead me to allow other people to make the investment decisions for me.

Knowing who I am increases my ability and effectiveness to be self-directed. Before I make any important changes to my family, education, career, or other aspects of my life, I have to know myself, in order to be true to myself. In order to know myself, I have to perform a self-assessment, by considering things I did or didn't do in my past, things I am currently doing, and an idea of the things I want to do in the future.

## 2. *What Qualities Do I Currently Have to Respond to Expected and Unexpected Challenges?*

In order for me to determine the qualities I have that allow me to respond to expected and unexpected challenges, I must perform an accurate self-assessment.

My self-assessment indicates my current level of my *self everything* such as my self-awareness, self-esteem, self-motivation, self-determination, self-confidence, and other "self" attributes. My self-assessment should be introspective and honest. I must be prepared for the revelation of both positive and negative abilities and limitations. Of course, it is easy for me to accept my positive qualities and abilities, but my acknowledgment of my negative qualities or lack of abilities is crucial and must be seriously considered before I make any changes in my life.

Am I am hopeful, or pessimistic? Am I stubborn, or open to accepting suggestions from others? Am I impulsive, or patient? Do I prefer the quick and easy way, or am I willing to invest time and effort? Am I money driven, or academic, desiring knowledge? Am I analytical, or artistic? Am I adventurous, or conservative? Am I determined, or do I give up easily? I must consider these characteristics as well as many others to get an accurate assessment of who I am.

For example, if I know I lack self-motivation, I must recognize that this limitation could present a challenge if I were to consider training to lose weight by myself. However, the acknowledgment of this limitation combined with my high desire to lose weight, presents me the opportunity to address my lack of self-motivation by hiring a trainer or getting a friend or family member to help motivate me to train.

This holds true for every aspect of my life: knowledge of self and the recognition of a limitation offers me opportunities to self-direct or proactively adjust. However, lack of knowledge of self or lack of recognition of a limitation increases my chances of finding myself in an unexpected situation where I will have to react to a challenge instead of proactively adjust. The opposite is also true: recognition of positive attributes or abilities can provide me with increased confidence, excitement, drive, and determination, along with reduced fear, to accept larger and more complicated changes in my life.

My basic self is my knowledge of self. It tells me who I am every day that I wake up. It informs me of my current abilities and limitations, which helps me gauge my confidence to respond to the expected and, most importantly, unexpected challenges in my life. Now that I have defined my basic self, I need an idea of where I want to go in my life.

## **_I Determine the Direction of My Life by Answering These Five (5) Questions:_**

### **_1. Where Do I Want to Go in My Life?_**

I must endeavor to live my life with focus and direction.

Clarity of purpose is my driving force, direction, or focus, where every major action I take will serve to satisfy that purpose. The highest form of clarity of purpose is my life passion. Passion is my ultimate motivational driving force and automatically includes clarity of purpose.

In order to live my life with focus and direction, I had to acknowledge my life has a grand design manifested by my passion or purpose. In its simplest form, passion or purpose is what gives my life a higher meaning and is the reason I do the things I do.

My passion or purpose has structure and is not haphazard in design and organization. As I shared earlier, there are many aspects of life, such as health, fitness, education, family, social, career, business, religion, art, science, music, and even love, just to name a few. The structure of my passion or purpose defines, organizes, and prioritizes the changes I make in my life. I also gain focus on the specific aspects of life to pursue or change in order to achieve my passion or purpose. My passion or purpose indicates where I want to go in my life. It is that which makes me want to get out of bed each day.

Sometimes, we do not know what our life passion or purpose is, or we thought we knew but changed our minds. This is OK. However, I strongly encourage you to endeavor to discover or re-discover it. If you do not know what your passion or purpose is or you need to re-discover it, you may get an idea of what it may be by taking note when you say things such as "I want to be…" or "I was thinking about doing this or that…"

Furthermore, you may discover your passion or purpose by asking yourself various questions such as "Do I want to be a professional athlete?" "Do I want to be married and have children?" or "Do I want to start a non-profit to help the homeless community?" Do you desire to become the next Bill Gates or Steve Jobs or get your doctoral degree in theology? What is the point of you going to work each day? What is the point of you joining the Peace Corp? What is the point of you volunteering at the Boys & Girls Club? What is the point of your fitness training and healthy eating?

18

What is the point of you going to college and earning your degree?

Simple or complex, your passion or purpose *is* the point because it continuously gives you the focus, direction, drive, and determination for everything you do.

Your passion or purpose does not have to be something tangible; it can be a concept or belief. For example, I grew up always being hungry and never getting enough to eat. Because of this, I developed clarity of purpose, which was comprised of various *nevers*, the primary of which was I *never* wanted to be hungry again.

If you have not discovered your life passion, it is OK. You can live a rich and rewarding life without ever knowing it. However, it is crucial to have a motivating driving force in your life, so I encourage you to endeavor to develop clarity of purpose for every important aspect of your life. Whatever you decide to do in life, do it to the best of your ability and with passion, purpose, focus, and direction.

### 2. *What Direction Is My Life Currently Going?*

I must endeavor to be aware of the current direction my life is heading.

While my life passion or purpose tells me where I want to go in life, sometimes I can get sidetracked. I am interested in many things in life, and not all of them are associated with my passion or purpose. My life will not and cannot be one-dimensional, only about satisfying my passion or purpose. My life must be multi-dimensional and include many activities, many of which are for the sake of enjoyment. There will be occasions where some of my decisions will divert me from my purposed path. One of the main benefits of knowing my passion or purpose is recognizing when the decisions I am making are moving me toward or away from my passion or purpose.

For example, consider that my purpose is to become a Fitness Boot Camp Instructor. At some point in my pursuit, I consider enrolling in a group fitness class or a beginner's guitar class. Acknowledging the structure of my purpose helps me recognize that the group fitness class progresses me toward my purpose and the guitar class, while interesting to me, moves me away from becoming a Fitness Boot Camp Instructor. While it can be both rewarding and acceptable for me to enroll in the guitar class, I must also be mindful that deliberately or inadvertently, pursuing a series of endeavors or making decisions that divert me from my purposed path can increase the time and effort required to return to and possibly achieve my purpose.

To illustrate this point further, imagine you are driving to a cross-country destination via an unfamiliar route requiring you to use a map. As you are driving your planned mapped route, you see signs or other indications along the way that give you the positive feeling that you are heading in the right direction. However, at one point, you are required to detour off your planned mapped route. As you are driving the detoured route, you begin to lose your positive feeling that you are heading in the right direction. You continue driving the detoured route. As you are driving the detoured route, a negative feeling completely replaces your positive, and you now feel strongly that you are heading in the wrong direction.

Based on this negative feeling, you pull over, consult your map, ask for directions, and make the necessary adjustments required to re-establish your positive feeling that you are heading in the right direction. This is similar for the direction of your life. When in tune with your positive feeling that your life is heading in the right direction, if, for any reason, you lose this positive feeling, you can quickly make changes to re-establish it with less time and effort.

In order to help me stay in tune with the current direction my life is heading, I developed my ***internal life compass***. My internal life compass indicates both positive and negative feelings that my life is moving in the right direction. When I am pursuing my life passion or purpose, my internal life compass will indicate positively that my life is heading in the right direction. However, if I pursue endeavors or make changes that divert me from my purposed path, my internal life compass will alert me that I may be diverting too far from my purposed path. When I am cognizant of the diversion, I will perform a life-direction assessment and make the necessary changes to return me to my purposed path.

Many situations can indicate reassessment, such as considering my current job a dead end, being involved in an unfulfilling or bad relationship, the inability to sleep due to the stress of dealing with the consequences and repercussion of impulsive decisions, the lack of excitement about anything or a general feeling of overall unhappiness with my life and other similar life events.

Positive situations can also indicate reassessment. For example, consider if my life passion or purpose is to open and manage five fitness centers, which requires me to work an average of twelve- to fifteen-hour days. During my pursuit, if I have an overwhelming desire to marry and start a family, this indicates reassessment is in order to balance work and home. Here's another example: consider that I am twenty five years old and I am on track with my purposed path to become a millionaire by my thirtieth birthday. While on vacation in Africa, I encounter a village of people who are struggling just to have clean water. This event reveals my previously undiscovered philanthropic and compassionate nature. The discovery of my philanthropic and compassionate nature could indicate reassessment in order to balance my desire to become a better human being, with my desire to become a rich human being.

### 3. Do I Make Good Decisions to Support My Life Direction?

I must endeavor to recognize and acknowledge that the changes or decisions I make today predict the path I will walk tomorrow.

Initially, this concept was both interesting and difficult for me to grasp. The changes I made earlier in my life interconnect with or influence my future options, decisions, or changes. I am sure you recognize that had I actually married and fathered six children at the age of sixteen years old, it would have definitely dictated a much different life path compared to when I didn't.

Sometimes the influence of my earlier decisions are not so apparent. For example, it took me years to recognize the probable interconnection between my desire to change my fitness at eight years old to be strong like my dad and my sixteen-year-old desire to become a dad. Many years later, after looking back and reflecting, it became apparent to me that my experiences as a son influenced my desire to become a father. Further, the awe and amazement that I felt when I saw my dad perform that feat of strength influenced my desire to be just like him. This event most likely influenced my desire for my child to want to be like me.

Regardless if the interconnection of my changes are apparent or not, I must continuously appreciate and be aware that the major decisions or changes I make or don't make continue to affect, define, redefine, and direct my life.

### 4. *Am I Reasonable with My Expectations?*

I must attempt to base my expectations on knowledge and understanding of what I want to do. Further, regardless of the outcome of my efforts, I must try to learn from my efforts and be gracious for the experience.

Most fitness and life endeavors are challenging, so I must be aware that real, sustainable, and maintainable change takes time, all of the time. Fitness and, to a greater degree, life, is about equity and balance. In order to have reasonable expectations, I must realize that all changes are composed of both positive and negative elements. Further, I must realize that those negative elements are vital for growth, maturity, and experience.

Fitness, in most instances, is adversarial. If my goal is to lose fifty pounds of body fat, acquiring knowledge and understanding regarding fat loss will help me understand that initially, my body will resist my efforts to reduce the calories I consume from simple carbohydrates (e.g., candy, cookies, cakes, pies, etc.). It is also reasonable to anticipate that my body may also increase its hunger cravings and mental cues telling me that losing body fat is too hard, so I should give up.

My increased knowledge and understanding gives me **reasonable expectations**, and reasonable expectations give me **patience**. In this example, increasing my patience should help me understand that it took time for me to put on the excess body fat, so it will take time for me to take it off.

If my efforts are purposeful and honest, then I must strive to be grateful and accepting of the outcome, especially when the outcome is less than I desired. I am a product of my thoughts. In general, I think we devote precious little time appreciating and being grateful for the positive aspects of our lives. I have been guilty of this many times over the course of my life, but I have grown and continue to grow to appreciate more of the good in me and surrounding me.

Even in defeat, when a change I attempted to make did not work out the way I planned, there is always good in the attempt. Seeing the good requires positive intent and active participation. In order to see the good, I must want to see it.

The challenge is for me to do my best and not let the negativity that surrounds me facilitate concentration on what I don't like about the world or my life, job, financial situation, or physical self. Positive or negative, the prevalence of my thoughts can have a cumulative effect. If I constantly think of what I don't like or don't have or the things I have not accomplished in my life, most likely it will result in a pessimistic or negative viewpoint. Further, when my disposition and expectations are not based on knowledge, understanding, and patience, it is reasonable that the changes I decide to make will materialize those expectations, and the results will be less than my full potential.

## 5. Am I Prepared for BOTH Expected and Unexpected Challenges?

I must recognize that my life is dynamic and change is inevitable. Therefore, I must continuously redefine my basic self **AND** confirm or correct the direction of my life.

Life is everything, and everything in life changes. Who I am will change based on my experiences, successes, and failures. I must always do my best to have an updated knowledge of self. I must redefine my basic self and replenish my positive personal foundation. I must acknowledge that my perception and perspective, whether positive or negative, influences the definition of my basic self. Acquiring and maintaining a positive basic self can be elusive because my mental disposition, positive or negative, is fleeting. Consciously or unconsciously, I constantly update my mental outlook. I am a product of everything that happens to me in my life, from the major change I make to the minor events of my day.

When I am in tune with myself, my perception to recognize the things that are changing or that I need to change increases. Further, my perspective becomes more sensitive regarding how I feel about the things that are changing or I need to change. Lastly, the changes I manifest through my actions reflect more accurately to my perception and perspective. All combined, my perception, perspective, and behavior help me redefine my basic self and determine my readiness and ability to facilitate or respond to change.

Additionally, after re-evaluation, if my self everything is mostly positive and my basic self or internal personal foundation is positive, I am confident that I am ready to accept the challenge, regardless of what I decide to change in my life,.

However, I am not perfect and never will be. There will be times when my basic self is mostly negative. When I recognize that I have a negative disposition, I have the opportunity to change something to increase positivity. Whether I assess myself as mostly positive or negative, I should always know myself, in order to be true to myself before I attempt to change myself, regardless of if the change is to my fitness or my life circumstances.

A major indicator of where the changes I make for my fitness or life pursuits will end is based on where I start. For me, starting from a place of passion or purpose, positivity, and confidence is preferred. Before I change anything, I must know what I am changing, why I am changing it, and the value of that the change to me. My basic self helps me determine this.

**Knowledge of self, combined with a passionate or purposeful direction for my life, increases my knowledge, understanding, patience, and confidence to change something about myself in order to become something else, to become a better me.**

Now that I know who I am and where I am in my life and I have an idea of where I want to go in my life, all I have to do is decide what to change to get there.

## *Reflections and Practical Applications:*

- Create your Personal Assessment:

Now it is time to take a good look at yourself and create your own personal assessment. It is important to be completely honest, as this information will help you understand who you are and where you are, so you can set appropriate goals for where you want to be.

Imagine that you are a being interviewed for a human interest story and are asked the following questions:

1. Tell us about yourself. What would you say?

2. What would you say are some of your best qualities?

3. What are the things that you can improve about yourself?

4. What is one of the best lessons that you learned from your past?

5. Are you happy where you currently are in your life? If so, why? If not, what can be done make it better?

# CHAPTER 2

*How To Determine The Difference*
*Between A Want And Need*

You may be thinking, OK, Carl, I have performed my personal assessment, defined my basic self, and have a good idea of who I am as a person, where I currently am in my life, and an idea of my life direction. So now what should I do?

I will answer this question at the end of this chapter. For now, I have two (2) questions for you. What do you want to do? What do you need to do?

Before you answer, consider the following encouragements.

## ***Determine Your Definition of "Want" and "Need"***

For me, there is huge difference between a want and a need. A want is optional, something that is nice to have. A need, on the other hand, is almost primal in nature, like oxygen, water, food, clothes, and shelter, something I will do whatever it takes to get. Deciding if something I desire is a want or a need can require serious thought and can be mentally taxing. In fact, this thought process is too mentally exhausting for me to perform every day for every desire. In order to keep myself from walking around every day taking every decision too seriously, I've learned to organize my desires and place them into one of two categories: life-altering or lifestyle.

Life-altering decisions are the serious decisions, the "needs," regarding career, relationship, family, medical, retirement, health and fitness, financial, and other such decisions. I definitely take the time to consider the seriousness of these decisions.

Lifestyle decisions are less serious, the "wants," such as the type of hobbies I engage in, the style of clothes to buy, entertainment when I go out, and other such things. These decisions take less time to consider because I already know the reason I want these things: because I want it. There is nothing deep or profound, I just want it. Sixteen-year-old Carl is still alive and well in me today with his "I want that, so get it" disposition.

We all have these wants inside us to some extent, so let me take a moment to emphasize that we must exercise caution with these lifestyle decisions. An abundance of decisions based mostly on "wants" can place you in undesirable circumstances. Regarding health and fitness, over-indulgence in foods high in trans fats or sugar and similar foods while of neglecting healthy vegetables, fruits, and other whole foods can lead to heart disease, diabetes, and obesity, among other health-related issues. In life, the "Keeping up with the Joneses" mentality or living beyond your financial means are lifestyle decisions that can lead to stress, financial ruin, bankruptcy, and a plethora of other negative finance-related situations.

I encourage you to take time to distinguish between your wants (lifestyle) and needs (life- altering) decisions. Once you can distinguish between the two, you can strike a balance to ensure that you do not over-indulge in lifestyle decisions. This balance will also reserve your serious thought-processing ability for life-altering decisions.

## ***Determine the Level of Importance of the Want or Need***

After I determine if my desire is a want or need, I must determine how important it is to me. My desire has varying levels, where the higher my desire, the higher the level of importance.

### **Importance = Time + Money + Effort**

I learned a long time ago that an indication of how important something is to me is the amount of my time, money, and effort I am willing to devote to it. This may also be true for you. Take a moment to think about a major goal you achieved. For comparison, now think about a major goal you did not achieve. Compare how much of your time, money, and effort you devoted to each. Regarding the achieved goal, you may discover that among other things, you devoted an appreciable amount of your time, money, and effort to the successful conclusion. Conversely, the amount of your time, money, and effort you devoted to the goal not achieved may have been less.

I have grown to trust that the amount of my time, money, and effort I invest indicates the probability of my success. However, it does not guarantee success. Even more predictive is that as I devote an increasing percentage of my time, money, and effort to a change, its level of importance to me increases. When the level of importance increases, especially approaching 100 percent, a previously defined "want" may transform into a "need," bringing with it the corresponding primal mindset that I will do whatever it takes to achieve the need.

In order to determine how much of my time, money, or effort I will devote, I ask myself these four (4) questions:

1. What do you want?
2. Why do you want it?
3. What are you willing to do to get it?
4. What value will it bring to you after you get it?

The more detailed my answers, the more accurate my assessment of how important something is to me.

Let us take a closer look at these questions. It is relatively easy for me to solve for "What do I want?" and "Why do I want it?" Answering these two questions also serves to provide another opportunity to ensure that I have categorized my desire into the correct category. However, accurately solving the questions of "What am I willing to do to get it?" and "What value will it bring me?" is more difficult, but VERY crucial.

## *Time for a story to illustrate my points.*

Earlier in the book, I told you about eight-year-old Carl, the little boy who had better things to do than help his father move stuff. Well, one of those things was playing the That's My Car! game with his friends. The object of the game was to "win" a cool car. In order to win the car, one of us had to be the first to see a cool car and then shout, "That's my car!" If more than one of us shouted, "That's my car!" at the same time, the group would decide who won that car and further, who had the coolest car to that point.

There were four of us, all sitting on the curb in front of my house watching with anticipation as cars went by. Let me tell you, there was a sense of excitement and pride to be the one with the coolest car. Over the years, whenever I remember this game, I always consider it interesting that even at eight years of age, we loved our cars, even if the cars were imaginary! As an extension of that game, I also fantasized that one day I would be sitting alone on the curb and a man with a cool car would actually stop, get out of his car, and say, "Here you go, bro," as he was giving me the keys to his cool car! I had a vivid imagination! (Note: I am going to talk about vivid imagination later in the book.) Of course, no one ever stopped and gave me a cool car, but this fantasy stayed with me and influenced me as I grew up.

Many years later, I was in Charlotte, North Carolina, on a work assignment. After a long day at the office, I was driving home as I normally did. On this occasion, however, I saw this car sitting on top of a hill at a car dealership. I remember that the hill was very steep and covered in very green grass. The car was parked in the downward direction as if it was about to drive down the hill to meet me. The car was also a convertible, painted white, and gleaming in the sun. I thought to myself, WOW, that car is beautiful. What is that? I had never seen a car like it before. A few days later, I stopped at the car dealership to take a closer look. The car was a Jaguar XJS, which I had never heard of before.

Now this car was in my consciousness, and further still, I could not escape thinking about it. I tried putting it out of my mind by telling myself things such as, "Carl, you don't need that car," or "Carl, save your money. You don't need to spend money on such an impractical car." Over the course of weeks I attempted other avoidance techniques, but they all failed. No matter what I did to avoid thinking about this car, I continued to feel that I wanted it! I could not stop thinking about this Jaguar. Therefore, my challenge became to determine if the car was a want or need, but most importantly, if this car was realistic for me.

I did a lot of research and found the price range of the car, which was high. The maintenance costs, even higher. Surprisingly, the insurance coverage was reasonable. However, the reliability, while not as reliable as I wanted, was not too bad. This car was the most expensive car I had ever considered purchasing. I analyzed all of this information and more to determine what the requirements would be for owning the car. I remember thinking to myself, "Carl, this is a very STUPID financial decision!" I also remember thinking that because I could not stop thinking about this car, perhaps there were unknown dynamics at play that were influencing me beyond the financial costs and subsequent fears associated.

Now that I had more financial information and still remained afraid of the cost of the car, I almost abandoned the desire to have it. However, I continued. During the process of deciding if this car was within the realm of my possibility, I discovered four important life tools: ***critical thinking***, ***calculated risks***, ***motivation***, and ***commitment***.

I discovered **critical thinking** and **calculated risks** as I was creating my primary, secondary, and since I was financially afraid, tertiary plan to purchase and pay off the car, all while meeting all of my other financial obligations. I also discovered the influence of **motivation** during my process of creating all of those plans.

Motivation gave me reasons why I should take action to buy the car. My motivation is comprised of many things. However, primarily, it is the answer to the questions "What do you want?" and "Why do you want it?" My motivation can be intrinsic or extrinsic. For me, the best source of motivation is intrinsic because it is internal, it originates from within me, and it is self-generating and self-replenishing. Extrinsic motivation originates from external sources, the outside world. It can come from your father, mother, coach, or spouse, among others. Extrinsic motivation can be just as powerful as intrinsic motivation, and in many instances you will need the external sources to replenish this type of motivation to an appropriate level in order to continue taking action. I encourage you to acquire and maintain an appreciable amount of both intrinsic and extrinsic motivation, but place a higher emphasis on internal motivation. I measure motivation in various ways: intensity, degree, scale (low to high). Regardless of my measurement method, the higher my motivation, the more likely that I will take action. Conversely, if I lack motivation, it will result in me abandoning the idea.

To continue the story. After creating my plans, I determined that I had motivation and solid plans to buy the car. However, I was still afraid as I remembered the old saying, "The best-laid plans of mice and men often go awry." This was a very expensive car, so I had to consider what I would do if my plans did not work as I imagined. What would I do if I lost my job? Perhaps the maintenance and insurance costs would become a larger burden than I expected. How would I overcome obstacles, with motivation? Most likely not. While I could remind myself of the reasons for buying the car, in order to overcome an obstacle, I needed more. I further imagined that if I spent money on a down payment, paid finance charges, purchased insurance, and the like, I would refuse to accept losing the money, time, and effort that I put into buying this car. These thoughts helped me discover **commitment**.

Commitment is the answer to the "What are you willing to do to get it?" question. Commitment is the "I will not be defeated" attitude manifested by actions and the refusal to let anything stand in my way. For me, my motivation and commitment are continuations of each other.

Simply put, motivation is the catalyst needed for me to start pursuing my goal. Commitment sustains me and is the fuel I need to overcome obstacles in order to continue the pursuit and potentially achieve my goal. My motivation and commitment must be dynamic in order to fuel and refuel me to overcome any challenges and obstacles encountered, until my goal pursuit is completed.

In my final analysis, I concluded that purchasing this car was a *want* and was well beyond the basic utility and practicality of a car. However, I also realized my desire to own this car could provide value beyond the car itself. If I decided to create the goal to purchase the Jaguar because the achievement of this goal would be emotionally rewarding, offering me an appreciable sense of fulfillment, accomplishment, and pride. As an added bonus, when I purchased the car, eight-year-old Carl was ecstatic because finally, HE was the man with the cool car, and that was immeasurable!

Now I will answer the question posed at the beginning of the chapter: So, now what should I do? My answer is simple: do what you are motivated to pursue and committed to complete.

## **Reflections and Practical Applications:**

- Time for the "Do you Want It or Need It?" Game!

  This game is designed to help you discover your definition of a need or want.

  Lucky you! You won the lottery. However, the amount of money you won is enough to make your life easier but not enough to retire.

  a.  Determine if the following are needs or wants:

      1.  Cosmetic surgery procedure which **may** increase your self-esteem.
      2.  Pay down the principle portion of your mortgage.
      3.  Manolo Blahnik Pumps or Hugo Boss Suit.
      4.  A luxury Mediterranean cruise.
      5.  Double your yearly contribution to your favorite charity.
      6.  New furniture.

  b.  Now take a moment to create your list of 5-10 items that you desire. Which are needs and which are wants, and why?

# CHAPTER 3

*How I Determine My Possibilities*
*From The World Of Possibilities*

In the last chapter, I encouraged you to do what you are motivated to pursue and committed to complete. This remains my encouragement. However, before you take action, consider your strengths and limitations.

We all have strengths—genetic, physical, educational, and so forth. We also have weaknesses—genetic, physical, educational, and so forth. The challenge for us all is to discern the difference. This is why knowing who you are by defining your basic self, which includes your strengths and limitations, is critical.

When I was in the ninth grade, I was fourteen years old and on the track team. My specialty races were the 440-yard and 880-yard dashes. On my track team, Jesse was the premier 440-yard-dash runner, and Ricky was the premier 880-yard-dash runner. Back then, the reality of the situation was that I was not fast enough to be the premier 440-yard- or 880-yard-dash runner. In my mind, though, my reality was that I believed in myself and that I could compete and win. I definitely had the positive personal foundation and self-confidence in abundance. I attended every track practice and even practiced on my own time with the desire to become faster. I did everything the coach asked of me in order to be on the track team. I remember thinking that I could win an actual track meet race in spite of the fact that during the track team practice, I could never outperform Jesse or Ricky. Regardless, my mind remained focused and positively thinking that all I needed was the opportunity to run during a track meet, and somehow, I would win.

One day, we went to a track meet and the coach put me in the 880-yard-dash race. I thought, finally, my time has come and I have my chance to win! Of course, prior to this, I had only run this race during practice. Regardless, I was supremely confident I would win. I was a little nervous, but I reminded myself of all of the things I did to prepare for this event. I remembered how I did my best during the track practices, practiced on my own, and did everything the coach asked me to do.

Finally, it was time for the race. In my mind, all I had to do was to run as fast as I could and I would win this race. It was simple: two times around the track. We lined up, the starter's pistol sounded, and I took off! I was amazing, leaving everyone behind me in my wake. At 110 yards and 220 yards everything went according to plan! At 330 yards, I began to have physical issues. What's this? My body was beginning to strain, but my mind was still confident, thinking that all I needed was for my body, my ability, to get back in synchronization with my mind. At 440 yards, one lap completed, I was slowing down and my competitors were gaining ground. I remember having the first realization that the race was not going as well as I imagined, and further, I may not win. The race continued. At 450 yards, I was sure I was not going to win. The race half over, at 500 yards, my speed was fading fast and my competitors had caught me. My mind definitely conceded that my plan was seriously flawed.

I began to accept the fact that my expectations, my goal of winning, were not realistic based on my ability. Confidence falling, at 550 yards, my competitors had overtaken me and were pulling away. I was exhausted and physically spent, and it felt like my heart was going to beat right out of my chest. I remember my last thought was that I was completely exhausted, then the unthinkable… "I QUIT!"

Take a moment and think about that. I quit the race WITHOUT finishing! I immediately felt embarrassed, defeated, dejected, humiliated, and like a complete failure. I remember walking off the track. I had to jump over a fence to leave the track and cross the infield in order to return to the section of the bleachers where my team was sitting. It seemed like it was a million miles away with all eyes in the stadium looking at me.

I am sure you can imagine that all of those eyes *were* looking at me in disbelief! When I finally made it to my team, the coach and my teammates did not speak to me. Their silence was deafening. Needless to say, the coach NEVER put me into another race. I lost his trust and respect, and the respect of my teammates. My track career was over.

To this day, I remember the embarrassment of my track meet failure as though it happened yesterday. Years later, this failure became a pivotal and eventual foundational learning moment in my life. I vowed (clarity of purpose) never to put myself in a position to quit as I did during that race.

As I reflect on this story, I remember that back then I was influenced by that old saying parents often say to their children: **"You can do anything you put your mind to."** Now, we all understand parents want their children to reach their full potential or endeavor to go beyond their current situation and aspire to do more, be more. While I agree with the sentiments of the saying, I do not agree with the saying itself. **To me, this saying is just not true and is a recipe for unrealistic expectations.** I know that while I can firmly believe "I can do anything I put my mind to" and I can also have a positive personal foundation and self-confidence, rest assured there are things I am not able to do. The reality is that I cannot do anything I put my mind to, especially if what I put my mind to is unrealistic. This is the flaw in that old saying. It is incomplete. I learned many things from my track meet failure as well as many other failures in my life. The most important lesson was that believing in myself, having a positive personal foundation, and self-confidence was not enough—I needed more.

My father said to me many times, "Boy, a man has got to know his limitations." I can't remember the situation when he first said this to me or if it was before or after the story I just shared. I do recall that years after my track meet failure and while remembering what my father told me, I gleaned his meaning for myself and concluded that my father wanted me to be realistic with the things I thought I wanted to do or could do.

How can I become more realistic? I wondered. I was not sure, but the first thing I did was change my perspective to recognize the fact that I can't do everything I put my mind to. I have limitations. Genetic limitations, athletic limitations, and a host of other limitations. I also have abilities. Genetic abilities, athletic abilities, and a host of other abilities. I will never know the full list of my abilities or limitations, so I will also never know the full list of my possibilities from the world of possibilities. Depending on what I am attempting to change about myself, a previous limitation can become an ability, and conversely, a previous ability can become a limitation. I find this fact about my life fascinating, because it gives me endless possibilities!

Sometimes, endless possibilities can be daunting and debilitating. In order to make my endless possibilities less daunting, I discarded the old saying, "You can do anything you put your mind to," and created a new saying by changing one word. I replaced the word *do* and with *pursue*. "You can pursue anything you put your mind to." To me, changing that one word made all the difference. *Pursue* grants me full access to ALL of the world's possibilities. *Pursue* also provides me the opportunity to endeavor to go beyond my current limitations and aspire to do more, be more, and possibly reach my full potential. *Pursue* does not guarantee success as the word *do* implies. *Pursue* means that I have the opportunity for success or failure, but most importantly, *pursue* offers me the opportunities to make adjustments along the way that could increase the probability of success. *Pursue* means my results will be based on my abilities and my situational assessment of my goal pursuit actions or inactions.

**"I can pursue anything I put my mind to."** This is an excellent positive starting point, but I still needed more to help me make better choices regarding what I wanted to pursue. My life is all about how I change myself to be different from what I currently am. In my track meet story, I needed to change my physical abilities to be able to compete and win a race. The same is true for changing from a high school graduate to a college graduate. Changing from a muscularly weak person to muscularly strong. Changing from an apartment renter to homeowner. Changing from a single man to a married man. Changing from an overweight diabetic to a normal weight non-diabetic. Changing from a personal trainer to a fitness consultant and business owner.

I change my life by pursuing who I want to be, which is how I turn my aspirations and possibilities into realities. However, I still needed a way to bring structure to the way I changed my life.

## *Reflections and Practical Applications:*

- Take a moment to think of an instance where you believed you could do something very challenging when others told you couldn't.

  a. Did you achieve the goal?

     - If yes, how did you overcome each challenge?

     - If no, what was the main cause of your failure and what would you do differently?

# CHAPTER 4

## Creating Attainable Goals

In the last chapter, I shared why I disagreed with the sentiment, "You can do anything you put your mind to." I also disagree with this sentiment: "I can quit anytime I want to." Alcoholics, smokers, gamblers, and others who are addicted respond this way when confronted about their addictive behavior. If I were an alcoholic, I imagine I would also believe that if I put my mind to it, I could quit drinking anytime I wanted to. While this may be true for some, you can research for yourself and find various studies and statistics that have repeatedly proven that for many alcoholics, relying on their mind or willpower to quit drinking is unrealistic.

Additionally, in the last chapter I said I needed a way to bring structure to the way I changed my life. This chapter focuses on creating realistic or, better yet, attainable goals. Similar to many people, fourteen-year-old Carl believed that all that he needed was his mind or willpower alone to make a goal of winning a track meet race attainable. While my willpower was very powerful and my confidence was high, I still needed more than that to make my goal of winning the race possible or, better yet, probable.

I have learned from my track meet experience as well as many others that, for me and for many people, the definition of an attainable goal is relative and dynamic and can be difficult to define. It became reasonable to me that if I or anyone consistently set unattainable goals, the probability would be high that those goals may go unrealized. As a Fitness Consultant, I repeatedly encountered clients with dispositions similar to that of an alcoholic, who over-estimate their abilities while under-estimating the challenges for their goal. The opposite is also true. I encounter some clients who under-estimate their abilities while over-estimating the challenges for their goal. Regardless of whether a person over-estimates their abilities or under-estimates them as they relate to the challenges for a goal, the result for both most likely will be sub-optimal performance resulting in the increased probability of their goal being unrealized.

While my disagreement with the two sentiments above may seem negative, the alternatives I will share can assist you with setting a more realistic tone for your future endeavors.

I can imagine that some of you may be thinking, "Carl, I don't agree with you. I *can* do anything I put my mind to, and on top of that, *if* I wanted to stop doing something, I could stop any time I wanted to!"

If you are one of these people, then I say to you, **EXCELLENT**! If you believe in your heart of hearts that you can do anything you put your mind to, then do it! Put your mind to something, take action, and pursue it until you do it! If you believe your mind or willpower is all you need, then it doesn't matter what I or anyone else thinks!

If you are one hundred pounds overweight and you believe that if you put your mind to it, you can totally quit eating sugar-laden fast foods, processed foods, and packaged foods, then I say fantastic, quit today, your body will be healthier for it!

If you are a fifty-year-old man and have never swum a day in your life, and you believe that if you put your mind to it, you can learn how to swim and then go to the Olympics and break Michael Phelps's world records, then I say to you, jump into the pool and start pursuing that goal!

If you have been smoking three packs of cigarettes a day for thirty years and you think you can quit anytime you want to and you choose today to totally quit, then I say fantastic!

If you are a thirty-five-year-old woman with a five-foot-four stature weighing 120 pounds and you believe that if you put your mind to it, you can become a middle linebacker in the NFL competing against men weighing three hundred pounds or more, then I say to you, suit up and take the field!

The world may try to tell you what you can or cannot do, but those are only words. It is up to you to show the world what you really can do. I encourage you to pursue your goal even when the world thinks it is unattainable, because ultimately, it only matters if *you* think your goal is attainable.

However, before you create and pursue your next goal, I encourage you to define what an attainable goal is for yourself. Now, before you say your definition of an attainable goal is "I can do anything I put my mind to," remember, those too are only words. While they are very powerful words, which can serve as the mental, internal, and emotional component for your self-confidence, in order to actually *do* what you put your mind to, you will need more. You will also need the physical, external, and performance component, which are your actions and abilities.

When I consider fitness goals, my genetic potential makes the definition of an attainable goal relative and subjective. Over time, by applying this consideration, I have created my definition for an attainable fitness goal. Life goals have the same consideration, whereas I utilize my basic self to help me define attainable life goals. I think it is reasonable for you to recognize the following:

**The successful completion of a goal has two (2) components:**

1.  **Mental** (internal: focus, motivation, determination, confidence, etc.)

2.  **Physical** (external: your actions and abilities)

For example, if I say I have the self-confidence to create a goal to win a 10K competition race in world-record time, in order to achieve this goal, my actions and abilities must match my words. If I say I'm going to get my master's degree in mathematics, then I have to take action and actually enroll in the program, perform all of the coursework, and pass all of the tests to graduate. In the simplest terms, in order to achieve my goal, my words (mental, internal/self-confidence) and actions (physical, external/actions, and abilities) must match.

Later in this chapter, I will share with you my definition of attainable goals and how to create and pursue them.

Before I do, I would like to discuss goals in general.

## ***Why I Create Goals in the First Place***

I have the ability to make an endless number of changes in my life, manifested by my endless possibilities from the world of possibilities. However, I can't pursue all of them at the same time. I need structure, focus, and something to give the possibilities I pursue meaning. I create goals for many reasons, but the main reason is to change my life based on my passion or clarity of purpose. Sometimes I create goals for curiosity, self-improvement, enjoyment, competition, fun, family, and a host of other reasons.

In fitness and in life, goals are generally a combination of *planned, unplanned, coordinated,* or *self-directed. Planned goals* are expected because I want to create them. *Unplanned goals* are commonly unexpected. An example of an unplanned fitness goal is if I had an unexpected medical scare, and as a result, I created a fitness goal with the hope of decreasing the probability of having another episode. Unplanned life goals are similar. If I were the victim of a natural disaster and lost all of my possessions, I would create life goals to re-acquire the lost possessions. In both scenarios, the events were unexpected, so the resulting goals were unplanned.

Planned or unplanned goals can further be *coordinated* or *self-directed. Coordinated goals* are goals I pursue in coordination with someone else. My efforts as well as the efforts of the other person dictate the eventual outcome of a coordinated goal. An example of a coordinated goal is marriage, where the success or lack of success of the marriage is dependent on the efforts of both people. *Self-directed* goals are goals where my efforts alone primarily dictate the eventual outcome.

This chapter focuses on **planned, self-directed goals** and the importance of applying reasonable expectations to your goals with the hopes of increasing the probability of a successful result.

Earlier, I shared that when I was young, I lived my life haphazardly. Many of my goals were desire driven and did not consider the grand scheme of my life. In order to introduce more structure regarding how I changed my life, I defined my basic self and endeavored to live my life with passion or clarity of purpose. When I have focus, the goals I need to create will become more apparent and meaningful. Regardless of why I create a goal, applying a structured approach can help me achieve those goals. Additionally, developing a systematic goal creation and pursuit process can continuously help me define or redefine my definition of an *attainable goal.*

Passion or purpose is unique for everybody. What is consistent for all is that clarity of purpose offers structure, focus, direction, and meaning, which can assist in converting possibilities into goals. Applying a systematic approach to goal pursuit can help you consistently create, pursue, and achieve your goals in order to satisfy your purpose.

Does that sound complicated? I hope not. If this does sound complicated, I submit to you that every day on a smaller scale, you have a sense of purpose when you organize, prioritize, and complete your daily required tasks. For example, consider that you have a Saturday to-do list that has ten items on it you must complete. In order to salvage and enjoy as much of your weekend as you can, you will organize, prioritize, and complete your list as quickly and efficiently as possible.

It is usually when we attempt to apply clarity of purpose on a grand scale that we make it more complicated than it really is. To illustrate how intuitive having clarity of purpose can be, consider if your purpose is to open your own French restaurant where you are the only chef. Based on this purpose, the structure would include two life aspects: education to become a chef and opening your restaurant. Further, the structure of your purpose would dictate the order in which to pursue the life aspects. It is intuitive and reasonable that you would become a chef first and then open your French restaurant. I think you would agree that it is counter-intuitive and unreasonable to open your French restaurant before you become a chef. Most tasks we perform every day have a similar intuitive thought process. To continue with the example, in order to satisfy the education life aspect and become a chef, you must apply and be accepted into the culinary arts program specializing in French cuisine. You must then pass all academic tests as well as prepare French cuisine to the standards of the culinary arts program. You would create a goal for each step. Your first goal is to apply to the program and pass all entrance exams for admission and acceptance into the program.

Once you become a chef, then you would focus on the business life aspect to open your restaurant. You would create and successfully complete goals to achieve the business knowledge to open the restaurant. You would achieve your purpose of being the only chef in your own French restaurant when you successfully achieved the two life aspects: education to become a chef and opening your restaurant.

## ***Types of Goals***

In general, there are three (3) types of goals: ***process***, ***performance***, and ***outcome***.

1. ***Process goals*** focus on your ability to **learn something**. In fitness, an example of a process goal is for you to learn the proper technique to perform a tricep dip. Another example of a fitness process goal is for you to learn how your body converts the food you eat into biomechanical energy to fuel your muscles. In life, an example of a process goal is to learn a foreign

language such as Spanish or to learn how to brew a micro-beer.

2.  ***Performance goals*** focus on your ability to **do something**. In fitness, an example of a performance goal is consistently exercising three days a week for forty-five minutes a day at a moderate intensity. In life, a performance goal would be for you to pass the driving test to get your driver's license. A life performance goal could also be to take a trip to Spain and immerse yourself in the culture in order to increase your fluency in Spanish. In this example, your performance goal leverages your process goal of learning to speak Spanish. It is important to recognize that goals can be separate and distinct; however, most often, goals are interconnected by our life purpose.

3.  ***Outcome goals*** focus on your ability to **compete against others**. In fitness, an example of an outcome goal is that you want to win the Boston Marathon. Another fitness example is that you want to win your division in the national powerlifting competition. In life, an example of an outcome goal is that you want to become the senior vice president, selected over all other candidates who applied. Another example of a life outcome goal is that you want to win the Austin, Texas, Salsa Dancing Competition.

You may have recognized that two of the three goal types are similar. Process and performance goals are similar because they are both self-determining. Self-determining means that process and performance goals are completely in your control, and further, your success is almost guaranteed, *if* you do what it takes to complete the goal.

Outcome goals can be more difficult. Actually, outcome goals are the most difficult goals because the successful completion of the goal is not in your control and definitely not guaranteed. Outcome goals are the goals where your abilities are in competition with other people's abilities. In some cases, you can perform to the best of your abilities and still not outperform someone else who is performing at a higher level than you are. In fitness and in life, every competition is someone's outcome goal. With outcome goals, the reality is that you can confidently believe you can do anything you put your mind to, but when talking about the desire of winning a competition, the other person you are competing against can confidently believe the same thing. Therefore, sometimes you'll win and sometimes you'll lose. The eventual result of an outcome goal isn't totally in your control as it is for process and performance goals.

I encourage you to recognize the different types of goals and set your expectations based on the type of goal you create. I hope you appreciate the fact that process and performance goals can make you a better you. They are the foundation for self-improvement. With process and performance goals, you are in competition with yourself, and if you do your best, regardless of the result, you will always win! You can never lose!

I also encourage you to recognize that outcome goals are the most challenging and most difficult to achieve. Outcome goals definitely require you to be reasonable in your expectations. There are many examples of outcome goals in individual sports, team sports, entertainment, music, and other competitive arenas. Outcome goals exist in every aspect of fitness and life that has a champion, winner, or place designator.

As you are already aware, fitness and life are not black or white. Regarding the types of goals, be aware that process and performance goals will transform into outcome goals if you add an element that competes with others.

For example, a fitness process goal to learn the correct technique to perform a Tricep dip can transform into an outcome goal if your goal becomes to learn the correct technique to perform more Tricep dips faster than your co-worker. Goals can be separate and distinct based on your general interest in something, such as a goal to learn how to play the piano because you have always wanted to learn. Or goals can be interconnected based on your life purpose of being a professional pianist in an orchestra. Process and performance goals have the potential to make you a "better" you in all aspects of life regardless of the result.

Regardless of the type of goal, I hope you are reasonable in your expectations. Earlier in the book, I shared how I based my expectations on knowledge, understanding, and patience. I also shared that my basic self is comprised of both abilities and limitations. Therefore, depending on the goal, previous abilities could become limitations, and previous limitations could become abilities. This is an example of the dynamic nature of life as well as the dynamic nature of defining what is attainable for you.

To illustrate further, take a moment and consider the different levels of your capabilities based on your age. Your capabilities at twenty years old were most likely youth and a lack of fear. Your capabilities at forty years old may be maturity, experience, and assessing calculated risks. It is reasonable for you to see that your definition of what is attainable is dynamic and determined by who you are as a person, where you are in your life, and where you want to be (e.g., the successful completion of your goal). At any given age, I encourage you to assess reasonably whether your current qualities are abilities or limitations for your goal.

## **How I Define an Attainable Goal**

My definition of an attainable goal is when I utilize my basic self to reasonably assess if my actions and abilities can eventually satisfy all of the requirements of the goal until goal achievement.

In my track meet failure story, I shared that I learned many things. The most important thing was that believing in myself and having a positive personal foundation and self-confidence was not enough. Over time, I determined that I needed to be better at creating and pursuing goals.

The first step is acquiring knowledge for the goal and the ability to apply this knowledge to determine if a goal is attainable for me.

So, what is *knowledge*? There is an old saying that "knowledge is power," and I definitely agree. When it comes to fitness and life goals, knowledge is **more** powerful when I make it personal, dynamic, and derived from information specific to my goal.

*Information* is the requirements regarding anything you want to pursue in health, fitness, education, employment, business, sports, and any other aspect of life. Everything you want to pursue in life has requirements, so you must meet those requirements to achieve your goal.

For example, if you want to become a ballerina for the Russian Ballet, you will have to meet the existing requirements of the Russian Ballet Company. If you want to be a professional baseball player for the Chicago Cubs, your performance must meet the requirements of the Chicago Cubs. The promotion at work you are thinking about applying for has requirements you must meet.

Regardless of your goal, you can discover the power of knowledge when you gain the ability to gather requirements for what interests you in any aspect of life. Knowledge becomes personal and dynamic when you can create attainable goals from those requirements.

## *How I Create an Attainable Goal*

1. I acquire the list for all of the known requirements for the goal.

2. I determine if I currently meet or can meet all of the known requirements of the goal.

   If I do not meet all of the known requirements, I have to figure out how to meet the requirements through education, training, or other means.

3. I create my **Goal Pursuit Plan**, which will eventually meet all requirements to achieve the goal.

   There are usually unknown goal requirements, discovered only when I pursue a goal. I must have confidence that I will satisfy the unknown requirements when discovered.

4. I determine if I have the time to pursue the goal.

For this point, consider this equation: $\mathbf{ATC = (24 - S) - RTT}$.

You may be thinking, "Carl, what does this math equation have to do with changing my fitness or other aspect of my life?" My answer: EVERYTHING! The fact of the matter is that we solve this equation every day! Allow me to explain the equation.

**ATC** is my *available time for change*. There are twenty-four hours in a day. Next, I determine the average number of hours I sleep each night **(S)** and subtract it from twenty-four hours. Finally, I subtract my *required task time* **(RTT)** for work, school, children, and other tasks I must perform. The time remaining is what I can utilize to change something about myself.

For example, if I sleep seven hours per night and work ten hours per day, then I have seven available hours per day to pursue a goal to change something about myself, where 7 = (24h - 7h) - 10h. Of course, over the course of my life, the amount of time I sleep and/or my required tasks will vary. For that reason, I must continuously re-calculate my *available time for change* when considering the time requirements for a new goal.

My challenge is always determining if my required tasks are actually required. It is relatively easy to determine that work or school are needs, but other tasks such as attending social gatherings can be challenging. We are all unique, so our available time for change is unique. Our lives are filled with tasks we perform every day, and we think most of those tasks are needs. I encourage you as I encourage myself to challenge the tasks associated with your job, school, family life, and a host of other activities. There are always things that are not as important as we think they are. This becomes apparent when you really want something.

For example, if you are considering buying new living room furniture and the cost stretches your budget 21 percent more than you wanted to pay. It is reasonable that when you are thinking of ways to fit the furniture into the budget, you will challenge the things you spend money on. Perhaps you may think, "I can afford this furniture if I don't go out three times per week." You may even think, "I can save money if I don't get my morning buttery caramel Frappuccino with extra whipped cream." The list goes on and on. The important point here is when you want something bad enough, you will probably figure out how to make time, get money, or apply extra effort for it.

5. I determine if I have the focus, confidence, motivation, determination, and time for the goal.

If yes, then the goal is attainable and I create the goal. If no, for whatever reason, then the goal is unattainable and is not created.

## **_How I Pursue an Attainable Goal_**

In order to pursue my goals consistently, I execute my Goal Pursuit Plan to start my goal pursuit, and continue until the goal is completed or achieved.

There are four (4) elements in the plan:

1. **Acquire** all of the goal requirements.

2. **Assess** my current ability to meet all of the goal requirements.

3. **Adjust** by determining how to satisfy the existing and new goal requirements.

4. **Apply** myself by taking action in order to meet all of the goal requirements until I achieve the goal.

So how do you define an attainable goal? While the concept of attainability seems intuitive and simple, the definition of an attainable goal can be anything but. If you seek assistance from others to help you with determining if your goal is attainable, I encourage you to get as many opinions as you need from sources you trust and respect. After considering all of the opinions of others, ultimately, you must determine if your goal is attainable yourself.

I strongly encourage you to get all of the known requirements of the goal first and then reasonably assess if you meet all of those requirements before you determine if a goal is attainable. If you do not meet all of the requirements, you have to determine if you can gain the ability to meet all requirements through training, education, or some other means.

I further encourage you to be reasonable in the assessment to determine if your internal (self-confidence) and external (action/abilities) can eventually meet all of the requirements of your goal. Your reasonable assessment is the application of your knowledge and understanding and the definition of *attainable*. Additionally, there may be unknown goal requirements discovered while pursuing your goal, so you must have confidence in your knowledge and ability by continuously acquiring, assessing, and adjusting to meet new requirements as well as continue to meet existing requirements for the achievement of your goal.

Here is an example to illustrate the ability to assess if a goal is attainable: Imagine a potential goal to travel across the country from San Diego, California, to Bangor, Maine. There is a plethora of information regarding the routes and distance via plane, train, or automobile. Further, there is an appreciable amount of information regarding hotels, restaurants, national parks, and points of interest, among other considerations. Knowledge begins as you start to **acquire** all of the requirements regarding the potential goal of making this trip. Further, based on this knowledge, you determine if you are still interested in the potential goal.

Your knowledge becomes more personal by **assessing** if you meet all of the requirements and then determining if you have to make any personal **adjustments** by creating a plan to address all of the requirements. After acquiring, assessing, and adjusting to address all of the requirements, you determine if you can create a plan to create, pursue, and achieve the goal.

If you decide to create the goal, you then **apply** yourself by executing your plan to meet all of the requirements of the goal with the intent of successfully achieving it. In this case, you **acquire** the requirements regarding the modes of transportation, and you decide you would like to drive. You **assess**, **adjust**, and **apply** your knowledge to this requirement by having a pre-departure inspection and maintenance service performed on your vehicle to ensure the vehicle is ready for the cross-country trip. You further decide the amount of time you have to complete the trip and whether you will make stops at points of interest along the way or take the most direct route. From this information, you request vacation from work. You calculate the expenses and ensure you have the funds to cover the cost of fuel, lodging, and food, among other considerations. Additionally, you consider the locations of hotels, restaurants, and fuel stations and plot your travel route accordingly.

You start to pursue your goal by embarking on your trip. After you start driving across country, you discover the dynamic nature of goal pursuit requiring your knowledge and ability to be dynamic as well. Consider this: regardless of the fact that you had the pre-departure vehicle inspection and maintenance performed, your vehicle can still break down. Where will you repair it, and can you afford the cost? If you encounter adverse weather conditions, which strand you at a hotel for an additional three days, can you cover these costs? What happens if you arrive at midnight in another city and discover your reservation was lost and, further, the hotel is overbooked. How do you respond?

These are all examples of how you can discover unknown requirements. In order for your goal to remain attainable, you must have the knowledge and ability to satisfy both the known and newly discovered unknown requirements.

In order for your goal to remain attainable, you must have the ability to **continuously acquire**, **assess**, **adjust**, and **apply** yourself in order to satisfy both the known and newly discovered requirements for the successful achievement of your goal. Your goal becomes unattainable when you cannot meet all of the requirements.

To illustrate, continuing with the previous example, if you are now halfway across the country and your vehicle has an unexpected catastrophic engine failure which requires a full engine rebuild, this will cost additional money and time. Your goal remains attainable, if you can pay for the engine rebuild and get additional time off work as well as make adjustments for all other time considerations. Your inability to meet the requirements for money and time renders the completion of your goal unattainable. This is the dynamic nature of goal pursuit and the dynamic definition of *attainable*. Your ability to acquire, assess, and adjust to existing and unknown requirements and your continuing ability to meet all of the requirements continuously redefines your goal's attainability. Your goal remains attainable only when you can continue to meet all goal requirements until goal achievement.

Adjusting to challenges is indicative of life in general, regardless if your goal is driving across country, adopting healthier eating habits to decrease complications of diabetes, starting your own business, going to school to obtain a degree, building your dream vacation home, completing the Boston Marathon, or any other goal. I encourage you to be aware of the fact that sometimes, regardless of how well you prepare at the start of a goal, new and unknown requirements may present, and successfully meeting all new requirements may be challenging. Many fitness and life goals are complicated, so the more reasons you have for your goal, the more commitment you have to figure out a way to overcome challenges.

I encourage you to recognize the fact that it is possible that a goal which was previously unattainable can become attainable, and conversely, a goal which was previously attainable can become unattainable. It is your ability to discern the distinction that makes all the difference.

The list of what is possible for you from the world of possibilities has not been written. From the vastness of the world of possibilities exists your world of possibilities.

**"You can pursue anything you put your mind to, especially when you believe it is attainable."**

## *Reflections and Practical Applications:*

- Creating Your Attainable Goal.

This exercise will help you to get familiar with the thought processes for creating an attainable goals to do what you want to do.

Think of two goals you'd like to reach, one fun and the other serious. For each goal, perform the following:

1. Write the things you need to do to complete your goal.

   If you are unsure, where can you go for help?

2. For each item on your list, indicate if you can or can't currently do that.

3. If you can't, write what you will need to do to be able to do it.

4. After you have completed steps 1–3, determine if you believe that you can achieve it.

   If yes, then your goal is attainable.

# CHAPTER 5

*Why and How I Never*
*Fear Goal Failure*

In the last chapter, I shared with you why I create goals, the goal types, my definition of an attainable goal, and my method for creating and pursuing my goals.

In this chapter, I will discuss the possibility of failure when pursuing goals. It is important to acknowledge that there is always a possibility that any goal can fail. My focus now is to discuss the fear of failure, its effects, and ways to minimize the impact. Even better still, later in this chapter, I will share my method that offers ways never to fail at a goal again! Hint, the operative word is *perspective*!

I know failure well, as I have failed many times in my life. In fact, my desire to mitigate the effect of past failures still influences me today. Earlier, I shared my ninth grade track meet failure, where I quit the race without finishing. Immediately after I failed, I felt embarrassed, defeated, dejected, and ashamed. What I did not share earlier was the internal and external toll the failure took on me for the rest of the ninth grade. Internally, I was mentally debilitated because I constantly reminded myself of my failure by replaying it repeatedly in my mind. I remained on the track team until the end of the season; therefore, externally, others constantly reminded me of my failure. My embarrassment and disappointment in myself left me with very little desire to pursue any other extracurricular activities.

To this day, I still remember the embarrassment and shame of that event as though it happened yesterday. I vowed never to put myself in a position to quit as I did during that race. My vow became a pivotal, life-altering, and maturational event that shaped the way I approach the goals I pursue. How I define, create, and pursue attainable goals helped me avoid embarrassment and shame in my endeavors. However, I still needed something else to help me mentally and emotionally address my past failures as well as mitigate my fear of failure for future goals.

As I lived my life, I had many experiences that helped me discover the *something else* I felt I needed to decrease my fear of failure. Interestingly enough, one of those life experiences came from an unexpected source.

It was February, cold outside, and my son was about five years old. Two months earlier, for Christmas, I purchased him a bike with training wheels. My son loved that bike, but after about a month or so, he started asking me to take "those things" off his bike. He was referring to the training wheels. As many fathers have experienced, it was time to teach my son how to ride a bike. As usual, I started teaching him by running behind him holding him up as he learned to steer, peddle, and maintain his balance. From my son's perspective, it is reasonable that this felt similar to the training wheels, and he started shouting, "Daddy, let me go, I can do it!" I said to him, "Not yet, baby," as I kept running behind him keeping him upright. However, my son kept shouting, "Daddy, I can do it!" Of course, I knew my son was over-estimating his ability and under-estimating my contribution. I knew that if I let him go, most likely he would fall. Supremely confident, my son continued shouting, "Daddy, let go, I can do it!" Eventually, I let him go, and as I am sure you can imagine, he started wobbling, and then, BAM, he fell!

For me, the impact of my baby falling on the street was visually traumatic. I saw my son lying on the street, with the bike on top of him. I ran to him looking for signs of injury. I checked for blood, but there was none. However, his foot tangled between the spokes of the tire made it seem as though he had twisted his ankle. This fall looked very bad, and I thought my son would quit. I asked him, "Baby, do you want to try again or go into the house?" Attempting not to cry and in his broken little baby voice, he responded, "I want to try again." WOW, the fact that my son took a fall like that but remained undeterred was impressive to me! Further, my son didn't view his first attempt as a failure. Actually, he was not counting attempts at all.

I realized that my son had no fear of failure. His desire to ride his bike without "those things" on it dominated his thoughts, and he was singularly focused and resolute in his desire. My son did what he needed to do to learn to ride his bike. Further, when he fell or stumbled, he was not embarrassed, depressed, debilitated, or the like. My son made an attempt, then another, and then others. With each failed attempt, I helped my son see what he did right. I also helped him make adjustments for the next attempt. With each attempt, he got better and better until finally, my son learned how to ride his bike exclaiming, "Daddy, I think I got the hang of it!"

Have you seen a three- or four-year-old child playing on a playground? Generally, playing is how children learn. They have no fear of failure; they just try to do whatever it is they want to do. If a child attempts to do something, falls, and cries, after you comfort them and if you allow, the child will most likely go back and try again. Children keep attempting whatever it is that interests them. Further, they do not count attempts or internalize a sense of failure or the fear of it. While I taught my son how to ride his bike, my son taught me the perspective of a child.

Over time, I remembered what my son taught me, and I attempted to apply it to address the mental and emotional toll of my past failures, including the track meet. My son's perspective actually helped me reconcile with my past failures, but I still needed more to address the potential of my future failures. Eventually, I found what I needed in fitness.

Fitness, in terms of strength training, taught me that in order for my body to have the potential to become stronger, training to failure or near failure is required. I adapted my training style to seek volitional failure, which is my ability to perform an exercise correctly with proper form until I can no longer do so. Further, at each training session, I always ask myself for just a little more than what I did in the last training session. This training style is the physical manifestation of failure.

To illustrate, if I walked for 1.2 miles on the treadmill yesterday, at which point I felt that I could not walk another step, then today, I ask myself to walk just a little more. Asking myself for a little more could be an additional step or an additional mile. If I collapsed performing ten push-ups last week, then this week, I will attempt to go beyond my previous failure point and try to perform eleven push-ups. It doesn't matter if I fail to perform the eleventh push-up. It only matters that I try and keep trying until I move past my previous failure point. A little more could be decreasing my 100-meter swim time by one-tenth of a second or by adding an additional twenty pounds on my bench-press attempt. There are many fitness goal examples such as to walk, jog, or run faster, or perhaps to become stronger in squats, bench press, or deadlifts. Regardless of the fitness goal, in order to increase my fitness level, my process is the same. I must train using correct technique until I fail, then ask myself for a little more until I overcome my last point of failure as I progress to reach my fitness goal.

Fitness taught me that asking for a little more defines my failure point and how to increase my level of fitness to move past it and progress toward achieving my fitness goal. Over time, I had a profound idea. I wondered if I could adapt what I learned from fitness and apply it to my life goals, taking into account the complexities of life goals. Unlike fitness goals, my life goals were more serious because the consequences and repercussions of failure had higher stakes.

I realized that I feared failure for many reasons, the primary being the embarrassment and other emotions I felt in my track meet failure. However, and most importantly, I also realized that I could not live my life with this fear, and further, I actually needed failure or the potential of it to show me my current limitations.

Eventually, I learned not to fear failure in any aspect of my life. I acknowledge that there is always the possibility of failure, and I respect it. I attempt to mitigate its possibility and effect by taking a more serious and preparatory disposition by knowing and improving my basic self, creating attainable goals, and being reasonable with my expectations. Most importantly, I know that regardless of the results of my attempt, I define failure and will not allow failure to define me. What is even more powerful is the fact that if I do my best in an attempt, successful or unsuccessful, I can learn from it. This can help me perform better in the next attempt as well as help me push beyond my last failure point. Asking myself to do a little more than what I am used to doing is a catalyst for growth, maturation, and experience in every aspect of my life. This is how I learned to respect failure and not fear it.

## ***Failure or the Fear of Failure Is Primarily a Product of My Mind***

Failure can be both mental, manifested through negative emotions, and physical, manifested through less-than-optimal performance, or injury. The emotional toll can stay with me long after any physical wounds have healed. Failure, or more specifically the fear of failure, can be very impactful to my life, as the emotional toll can rob me of my adventurous spirit or the motivation and willingness to take action or create challenging goals. The fear of failure can also move me toward a safe, conservative approach to my life by causing me to avoid challenges or risks that if conquered could add more reward and spice to my life.

If you are concerned with past or current failures or have a fear of failure in the future, I encourage you to recognize that your perspective of failure and its effects are by your own design. The good news is, this also means they are modifiable, because failure is what you believe it to be. I encourage you to respect the possibility of failure and endeavor to reduce its effects by viewing it similarly to the way a child would: the result of a try. **If you try your best and do not succeed, if it is important to you, try again until you achieve.** I know this statement seems simplistic, but it is also true.

Earlier, I shared with you that your mind is very powerful and can provide a positive foundation for your self-confidence and self-esteem. When you decide to do something, **a mentally positive perspective can be your ally**. However, you must also be aware that fear of failure, fear of embarrassment, fear of disappointing your family, friends, or teammates, and doubt, indecisiveness, and a host of other similar thoughts can serve to decrease your motivation and self-confidence and lower your self-esteem. With a **mentally negative perspective, your mind can be your adversary**. It is possible for your mind to view the mitigation of failure as invigorating, or conversely, your mind can view the fear of failure as debilitating. You will never encounter a greater ally or more formidable adversary than yourself! The choice of perspective is yours to choose; however, sometimes, with choice, comes change.

For me, change is my ability to act or become different in some way, or an alteration of how I think or feel about something. For years, my mind was my adversary and fueled my negative perspective of my track meet failure. My son as well as other life events helped me choose to make my mind my ally. The choice to make my mind my ally required me to change my perspective. Changing my negative perspective was very difficult, but over time *and* after many attempts, I did it. Because of what I have experienced in my life, it is reasonable to me that you may find yourself in a similar position, where you may need to change a persistently negative mental perspective or physical behavior.

The next chapter shares with you how I change my negative perspective or behavior, with the hopes that my encouragement can help you change your negative perspective or behavior if or when you ever desire to do so.

## *How I Never Fail at a Goal*

The considerations I am about to share can be applied to simple goals, such as learning how to prepare an egg over easy without breaking the yolk, or complex goals, such as lowering your stored body fat while maintaining your lean muscle. Complex goals may be comprised of many elements, while simple goals may have only one element.

When you pursue a goal, on the highest level, the result can be success or failure. However, in order to minimize the effect of a failed goal, it may be helpful to view a goal on a more detailed level. At the lowest level, every goal, simple or complex, is comprised of one or more performance actions that you must successfully complete in order to achieve the goal.

Regardless of if the performance action is part of a complex goal or not, each performance action starts with a single attempt. This attempt can be successful or unsuccessful. Of course, the more challenging the goal or action, the higher the probability that some performance actions will require multiple attempts for you to become successful and achieve your overall goal. The excellent news is that in order to achieve your goal, you can have as many attempts as you need. However, in the event that you have an unsuccessful attempt, it may be helpful if you have effective ways to minimize any negative feelings.

The primary way I minimize the feelings of failure is to recognize there is value in an unsuccessful attempt. Every attempt, successful or unsuccessful, will offer lessons learned. Usually, an unsuccessful attempt offers more lessons, as it indicates a higher level of difficulty, which moves me closer to my current ability limits. If I am attentive to learn from the lessons offered, unsuccessful attempts can also be the catalyst for adaptation for my next attempt. Another way I minimize the effects of failure is to know that if my attempt is unsuccessful, I have options for responding.

## *Three (3) Responses to an Unsuccessful Attempt*

The responses to an unsuccessful attempt are to **adjust**, **redefine**, or **finalize**. Each response will have a different effect on the success or failure of my overall goal. I will explain each response in more detail below:

1.    **Adjust** to it by considering the lessons learned. Make adjustments as needed, and then apply any adjustments in the next attempt.

Adjustment to an unsuccessful attempt allows my goal pursuit to continue, especially when my perspective regarding the unsuccessful attempt is similar to that of a child: it is the result of a try. If I try my best and do not succeed, when my goal is important to me, I try again until I achieve. The knowledge I learn from the lessons will assist me with making adjustments and then applying the adjustments to the next attempt. The adjustments can also increase the level of my current ability limits and move me closer to achieving my overall goal.

2.  **Redefine** my goal after an unsuccessful attempt based on the lessons learned.

Redefinition of my goal after an unsuccessful attempt allows my goal pursuit to continue, pause, suspend, or transform. Goal redefinition can be difficult for many people because it requires the acknowledgment that under the circumstances, you cannot satisfy the goal's requirements. This is when you must recognize that your attainable goal has become unattainable. When this happens, I encourage you to remember that life is dynamic, so your response to life must be dynamic as well. Most goals take time to complete; some complex goals can take years to achieve. Until goal achievement, you must acknowledge that the circumstances at the commencement of your goal most likely will change during the pursuit of your goal. Your goal pursuit plan, mentioned in the last chapter, can help you adjust to the dynamic nature of life.

The first challenge that I had and many people may have is getting over the disappointment regarding the goal becoming unattainable. I encourage you to accept as I did that attainable goals can become unattainable based on circumstances outside of your control. Many factors can affect your goal pursuit, such as time requirement, finances, children, family, health-related issues, and a host of other things.

The takeaway here is that goal redefinition offers you unlimited options. You can redefine your goal in various ways. One, you can redefine the completion time parameters of your goal. For example, you are preparing to buy office space for your market analysis business, but two weeks before closing, your major investor backs out, dictating you acquire your office space the following year. Two, you can redefine the objective of your goal. For example at the start of your college education, your objective was to become an anesthesiologist. However, after three years, your focus changed to podiatrist. Three, you can suspend a goal. Your goal is to compete in the judo competition, but one week before the competition, you discover you are pregnant. You suspend your goal until some date after your baby is born.

Life is everything, and everything in life changes. You may have to redefine your goal based on health, family, work circumstances, or other reasons, both within and outside of your control. Regardless of the reason to redefine your goal, I strongly encourage you to recognize that the redefinition of your goal is your most powerful response option to prevent goal failure. The redefinition of a goal takes into account the dynamic nature of your life. Simply put, you must be adaptable to the changes of life, so your goals should be adaptable as well.

**3. Finalize** my goal after an unsuccessful attempt.

**Goal failure is final only when my failed attempt is my last attempt.**

If I decide not to adjust or redefine my goal after an unsuccessful attempt, then I have failed at my goal. Fourteen-year-old Carl failed at his track meet goal because he finalized his goal when he decided that his unsuccessful attempt was his last attempt. However, all was not lost. Later in my life, I gained knowledge from the lesson learned from that failure, adapted, and became more mature, along with a host of other positive attributes. I strongly encourage you to recognize as I did that **even in failure there can be victory**!

How do you define failure? How does failure make you feel? While failure seems negative, if properly considered, failure or the desire to avoid it can assist you in taking more serious and comprehensive preparatory actions before you pursue your goals. I encourage you not to fear failure; instead, respect it and embrace it. We need failure for many reasons. The most basic is to appreciate success. In order to help minimize negative effects, consider that failure offers us the opportunity to adapt, become more knowledgeable, and become stronger in our will and determination, as well as a myriad of other ways. Recognize that there is good in failure, and always try to find the good.

Most importantly, you determine the positive or negative effects of failure. Based on your perspective of failure, your mind can be your ally or your adversary. I strongly encourage you to make your mind your ally.

### **Reflections and Practical Applications:**

- How Do You Define Failure?

This exercise will help you review "lessons learned" from previous failures. It is my hope that the lessons learned will assist you with anticipating and preventing similar challenges with your future goals.

1.  Think of something you attempted and failed.

    a.  How did it make you feel?

    b.  How did you deal with any negative feelings?

    c.  Did you give up or did you try again?

    d.  What adjustments did you make for your next attempt?

    e.  What experience did you gain from the failure?

# CHAPTER 6

*How I Change My Perspective or Behavior*

In the last chapter, I shared with you that failure is based on your perspective. The reality for many, including myself, is that changing a perspective or behavior is very difficult.

In this chapter I will share how I change my perspective and behavior.

## *In Order to Change My Perspective or Behavior, I Must Be Self-Aware*

When I am self-aware, I am proactive to change and self-directed with my responses. Change influences my **perception**, which influence my **perspective**, which influences my **behavior**.

In order to increase my self-awareness, I have to ensure that my assessment of my basic self is accurate based on confidently knowing who I am as a person, where I currently am in my life, and where I want to go in my life. As I shared with you earlier, my self-awareness is a component of my basic self and helps me to be conscious of the need for change.

Self-awareness awards me with the opportunity to become self-directed and the ability to create and, to some degree, control how I change my perspective, behavior, or circumstance.

## *I Must Perceive a Potential Need for Me to Change*

I am a creature of my behaviors or habits, so before I can seriously consider changing anything, I have to become aware that I need to consider changing.

For example, if I gambled a lot, based on my negative behavior when I lose money, other people could likely conclude that I have a gambling problem and, further, that I need to change to address the problem. However, until I acknowledge that I have a gambling problem, it is reasonable that I will not change my behavior. Even if I tried to change to please others, most likely, I would put very little effort, if any, into changing.

There are many ways to become conscious of the need for a change. Sometimes it comes from the people closest to us. For me, I usually come to the realization that I need to consider changing when my mind and spirit are not at ease. Allow me to explain. I have a guiding force, which is comprised of my mind and spirit. My mind and spirit are fraternal twins, where my mind is the logical, analytical, action-oriented, task-executing part of me, and my spirit is the conceptual, emotional, sensitive, homeostatic part of me. Simply put, my mind tells me what to do or what not to do, and my spirit tells me how I feel about what I did or did not do. In order for me to acquire and maintain peace of mind, my guiding force must by synchronized, balanced, and at ease. I become aware that something needs to change when I have lost my peace of mind.

Some people call their guiding force their *intuition, inner voice*, or *heart of hearts*. I encourage you to determine if you have a guiding force, and if you do, be in tune with it. Your guiding force can assist you in making difficult decisions as well as let you know when it's time to consider a change.

The fact that you need to consider a change can show up in other ways as well. If you get headaches on Sunday afternoons because you dread going to work on Monday, it could indicate that you need to change something. If you routinely have the same nagging feeling that you are not happy with where you live, it could indicate that you need to change something. If you tend to see the bad in everything and everyone, it could indicate that you need to change something. If you have no drive or motivation to do anything but you are complaining about everything, it could indicate that you need to change something. Anytime you persistently and consistently have the same or similar negative thoughts about something, it is a good indication you should consider changing.

## *I Must Determine Reasons to Change AND the Benefits of Changing*

Changing a negative perspective or behavior is seldom easy. In fact, the more difficult the change, the more difficult the challenges I must conquer to facilitate the change. This is true for modifying any negative perspective or behavior.

Changing something about myself that I am used to doing or thinking is challenging. The challenge exists for me whether I am changing my negative perspective of my health and fitness or decreasing my behavior of procrastination. I should expect difficulties whether I am making a goal to decrease the number of sweets I consume, quit smoking or gambling, or a plethora of other undesired thoughts or behaviors. I know that for me to seriously consider changing, I need reasons to change and to get value for my efforts.

In order to prevent myself from abandoning the potential perspective or behavior change, I must immediately think of at least one major benefit for the change. In order to continue serious consideration of the potential change, I need to recognize as many benefits for the change as possible. Therefore, I create my **"Benefits from Changing"** list.

The best way for me to create my "Benefits from Changing" list is to compare my current perspective or behavior with the potential new perspective or behavior. The result is a detailed list of reasons for me to change or perhaps not change. Depending on the potential change, creating and documenting the "Benefits from Changing" list can take minutes, hours, days, weeks, and sometimes even months to complete. I will most likely know and accept that

I need to change when my reasons for change significantly outweigh the reasons not to change.

Regardless of the change, if I perceive the change to be difficult, I must prepare myself mentally as well as physically with the knowledge that I must take definitive actions to overcome the obstacles to change. Most importantly, I recognize that change does not happen overnight. The more reasons I have for the change, the better, because I know that if I decide to adopt a new perspective or behavior, when the effort to change becomes difficult, I can refer back to my "Benefits from Changing" list, which motivates me to persevere.

### *I Must Assess my Initial Motivation to Change*

At times, many people, including me, find change too difficult or lack the motivation to seriously try to change. Because of this, we keep doing what we've always done. Change usually comes when it becomes too painful, negative, or destructive not to change. When considering change, I have to determine if I have the ***minimum essential motivation to change***. I can say to myself, "Carl, you need to change this or that, and here are all of the reasons you need to change and the benefits for changing," but if I do not have the minimum motivation to change, most likely I will not even try. Further, even if I do try, it is probable I will not put enough effort into trying to change.

To illustrate, say I felt a tightness in my chest and decided to go to the doctor, and the doctor advised me that I had a minor heart attack and further directed me to change my nutrition by lowering my sodium intake and eliminating fried foods and saturated fats. If I determined that the value for changing was not enough for me to eliminate all of the delicious food I enjoyed, most likely, I would not have the minimum essential motivation to change. If instead of a minor heart attack, I had a massive heart attack that resulted in me having open-heart surgery, most likely my motivation level would exponentially exceed my minimum essential motivation to change.

## *I Must Determine How to Change*

When I decide that I want to change something about myself, the first thing I have to accept is that what I am currently doing is not good enough to achieve what I want to do.

Figuring out how to change a negative perspective or behavior can be very difficult. I must increase my knowledge and understanding regarding what is required for me to change and my ability to meet those requirements, set reasonable expectations, and be patient during the process.

While it is possible to determine how to change on my own, in order to increase the probability of success, I need to share my burden and create a support system.

My support system starts with the people who are closest to me: my family or friends who care for and love me. I can also find support from counseling professionals, help groups, organizations, and other sources I trust. Depending on the change, I may need support from one or more sources. In order to get the help I need, I have to be as open, honest, and vulnerable as I can when sharing my struggle. With the help of my support system, I can determine how to change and create my ***Change Plan***.

A *Change Plan* is, like it sounds, a plan for creating change. For example, if I wanted to lose body fat, my Change Plan would include the following steps:

1. Get as much information on my own regarding nutrition and body fat loss.

2. Speak with or hire a dietitian to get a nutrition plan for losing body fat.

3. Speak with or hire a personal trainer to get a fitness program to support my fat loss goal.

4. Ask my family and friends for support of my nutrition and fitness training plan.

## *I Must Re-Assess My Motivation to Change*

After I have acquired the knowledge and understanding to create a Change Plan, I must re-assess my motivation to change. I encourage you to recognize that in order to change something about yourself, you have to want to change. The more reasons you have to change, the higher your motivation will be to make attempts to change. Once you acknowledge this, you must meet or exceed your minimum essential motivation to change.

## *I Must Take Action and Execute My Change Plan*

In order to change, I have to take action and execute my change plan. I have accepted that change does not happen overnight. From start to finish, for all perspective or behavior changes, I have to meet or exceed my minimum essential motivation for change. Ultimately, my motivation and determination to overcome all obstacles and stay the course determines my success or failure to change.

However, even when my determination and motivation is high, I may still need ongoing support.

To illustrate, imagine that someone that you love needed your help to change his or her behavior to overcome drug dependency. I am sure you are aware that overcoming a drug addiction is not an overnight effort. As your loved one is battling the drug addiction it is reasonable that throughout their ordeal, you would give as much patience, understanding, and forgiveness as needed in order to help him or her overcome the addiction.

When I execute my change plan, I have to remember that change can take time. Most importantly, I know it is a process that may require many attempts. If I have a setback, I try to treat myself as I would treat someone I love, with patience, understanding, and forgiveness.

As long as I am taking positive steps toward the desired change, I will keep trying. Changing a perspective or behavior is difficult, so I continue to refer back to my reasons for change and continue to be open, honest, and vulnerable when sharing my burden with my support system. If I find that I just don't have the motivation, I have to recognize that I can't do it alone. I have to ask for help. I can confide in someone that I trust who won't judge me and can suggest "mini goals" with rewards as I satisfy each mini goal. Sometimes all I need is a kind word or understanding from someone I trust to help me overcome the challenges to change and persevere.

## *I Must Sustain and Maintain my Changed Perspective or Behavior*

After successfully executing my change plan, I must maintain the change. We are human, so it is possible to relapse back to old negative perspectives or behaviors.

Maintenance of a new positive perspective or behavior requires active thought and participation by acknowledging the possibility of relapse and taking preventative steps to avoid it. I maintain my positive perspective or behavior by referring to myself as *recovering*. For example, I would refer to myself as a recovering alcoholic and avoid hanging out in bars or other locations where alcohol flowed freely. I would refer to myself as a recovering fast food eater and avoid going to fast food restaurants to have lunch.

**When I am self-aware, I am proactive to change where I anticipate, manage, and direct my responses: Change begets Perception begets Perspective begets Behavior.**

Self-awareness awards me with the opportunity to become self-directed, which grants me the ability to create and to some degree control my change of perspective, behavior or circumstance.

## *Reflections and Practical Applications:*

- Is it Time to Change Something?

1. Think of something you may be interested in changing about yourself.

2. Write down as many reasons as you can why you should change.

3. Write down the benefit(s) if you changed.

4. Review your list reasons and benefits and determine if you want to make an attempt to change.

5. If yes, create your Change Plan:

    a. Get as much information as you can about the requirements to change.

b.  Tell your family and friends about your desire to change and ask for support.

c.  If you need additional information, ask other people you trust for help.

6.  Review your change plan and reasonably estimate the challenges to change and then determine if you still want to make an attempt.

7.  If yes, commit to executing your Change Plan to the best of your ability.

# CHAPTER 7

*Putting It All Together*
*With The 8 Pillars Of Goal Pursuit*

W hat do you want to be when you grow up? This question introduces the concept of change to children by asking them to think about being something different from what they currently are.

"Tell me about yourself," is often asked during a job interview. The list of questions you may be asked over the course of your life can be extensive. What are you going to do when you graduate high school? Are you going to college? Do you want to remain single or get married?

Regardless, if someone asks you these type of questions or you ask yourself, you can find the answer by knowing your basic self. Further, if you learn from your life lessons, your knowledge, understanding, patience, confidence, and other things mature as you mature. Forty-year-old you is more knowledgeable than twenty-year-old you, but may be less knowledgeable than fifty-year-old you.

I encourage you to know yourself in order to be true to yourself. We all have abilities and limitations, but it is the acknowledgment of both that helps with the attempt to become a better version of ourselves.

Your life is continuously changing, so seek a little more wisdom, a little more maturity, knowledge, understanding, patience, kindness, forgiveness, and empathy for both you and others.

Endeavor to become self-aware and self-directed for the major changes in your life by focusing on the things that matter most to you. Take time to determine why those things are important and the value they will bring. The more important something is to you, the more motivated, determined, and committed you will be to it. Being armed with the knowledge of self and a sense of your life direction makes you more mindful and purposeful for the decisions you make.

Your mind can be your ally or adversary. Your mental disposition determines which and is the foundation for all you desire to do. Every thought, positive or negative, affects your mental disposition. I encourage you to choose to see the positive while acknowledging the negative; it is an opportunity for growth. It is our ability to learn from the triumphant and tragic events of our lives that is invaluable.

Don't fear failure; respect it and mitigate its probability by setting reasonable expectations and attainable goals. If you fail, remember that failure can help make you better. We are not perfect and never will be, but we can all try to be better today than we were yesterday. Seek positive progression, not perfection. Our perspective is the key. Sometimes in order for us to get where we want to be in our lives, the most difficult change we have to make is to our minds to leave where we currently are.

With the purpose of encapsulating all of the considerations and encouragements I shared in this book, I offer you the secret of my success.

## **_The Eight Pillars of Goal Pursuit:_**

- **Pillar 1: Think It**

  Every day, I have many thoughts that bring something into my consciousness. Most are transient and dissipate just as fast as they are formulated.

  However, in order for me to change something about myself, I need **inspired thought**. Inspired thought has more substance and engages my mind to a higher degree. Inspired thought can originate from various sources, such as a person, a place, a thing, television, books, and music, just to name a few. An inspired thought is a potentially impactful thought that can change my life because it can be the catalyst for me to do what I am inspired to pursue.

- **Pillar 2: Believe It**

  As my inspired thought matures, I must increase my knowledge and understanding. What do I want to do? Why do I want to do it? What are the requirements to do it? Do I have the ability to pursue it? What value will it bring me if I achieve it? As I determine the answer to these and other questions, I may begin to believe that I can do it. The higher my belief that it is attainable, the more motivation and focus I have to do what I am inspired to pursue.

- **Pillar 3: See It**

  As my belief and confidence increases, I begin to "see" myself doing it, being it, or enjoying it. My **vivid imagination** helps me visualize the physical manifestation of the inspired thought. If I am inspired to open a fitness studio, I see myself in my studio training clients. The more vivid my imagination, the higher my motivation, determination, and commitment is to do that which I am inspired to pursue.

- **Pillar 4: Say It**

  Think It, Believe It, and See It are all internal pillars. Say It is the first external pillar.

  Telling others of my inspiration to do something is the initial indication of my passion or clarity of purpose. The more people I confidently tell what I am inspired to do also indicates my willingness to be accountable, not only to myself, but also to others.

  This **external accountability** serves to fuel my determination and commitment to do what I am inspired to pursue.

- **Pillar 5: Pursue It**

  Pursue It means to do it! This is the actionable pillar where my words and action increasingly match as I do what I am inspired to pursue.

- **Pillar 6: Adjust to It**

  Life is dynamic, and I accept that achieving what I am inspired to pursue will be challenging, with obstacles, trial, and tribulations. When I encounter challenges, I look "backward" to overcome them.

  When I look backward, I remember what inspired me, my belief in myself, and the mental images and imaginations showing me the results of my efforts. This helps increase my knowledge and understanding as well as my creativity to apply it to overcome all challenges.

  All pillars are always present in me, and depending on my need, allow me to shift my focus from one to another to get what I need to continue to do what I am inspired to pursue.

- **Pillar 7: Complete It.**

  **I will never quit my goal pursuit again.** I further commit to myself that every goal I pursue will be attainable based on my accurate assessment of the goal requirements and my abilities to meet all of them.

I will take every goal to its pursuit conclusion and accept that my goals may be achieved, redefined, or failed based on the dynamic nature of my life.

- **Pillar 8: Appreciate It.**

Regardless of the outcome of my goal pursuit, I am **ALWAYS** a better version of myself because of it. I gain experience and maturity from the lessons learned as a result of pursuing what I was inspired to do.

I live my life passionately, purposefully, and mindfully. I know where I want to go in my life, and I have an appreciation for where I've been. My life is not one dimensional but multi-dimensional, as I enjoy many things that bring wholeness and substance to my existence.

I have a guiding force supported by the eight pillars, to which I am in tune and trust. My guiding force directs and influences the direction of my life. Most importantly, my guiding force gives me inner peace and confidence to know when I am making the correct decision for a major event in my life.

The experiences and lessons learned from the eight pillars redefine my basic self as well as replenish my passion, purpose, knowledge, understanding, reasonable expectations, patience, confidence, motivation, determination, commitment, creativity, strategic planning, and many other things, which sustain and enhance me as I pursue those things that are important to me.

Who am I? I am he who is greater than the sum of his experiences indicates him to be.

**Who are you, where you are currently, and where do you want to go in your life?**

# About The Author

Carl Hunter is certified as a personal trainer with the National Strength and Conditioning Association (NSCA) and the World Instructor Training School (WITS) certifying authorities and has been a Fitness Consultant for over fifteen years. Carl specializes in a holistic approach to health and fitness, which includes nutritional counseling, strength training, cardiovascular and pulmonary training and both physical and mental rest and recovery strategies.

Additionally, Carl is an instructor for the University of Texas (UT) Personal Trainer Certificate Program, where he instructs personal trainer students regarding how to apply their classroom knowledge practically in a hands-on manner. Carl is also on the staff of the University of Texas Health and Wellness Department, where he trains faculty, staff, and students, as well as mentors personal trainers new to the department.

Carl has also been a Computer Analyst Consultant for over twenty-five years specializing in the maintenance, repair, and enhancements of business systems. Carl has worked with companies such as Shell Oil, Texas Instruments, Transamerica Reinsurance, Blue Cross Blue Shield of Ohio, and the Chicago Mercantile Exchange, just to name a few.

Made in the USA
Middletown, DE
06 September 2018